Ocean

LIVE. LEARN. DISCOVER.

Bath · New York · Singapore · Hong Kong · Cologne · Delhi · Melbourne

First published by Parragon in 2009

Parragon
Queen Street House
4 Queen Street
Bath BA1 1HE, UK

ISBN 978-1-4075-8088-3
Printed in China

Contents

Rocky shores

When beaches are covered with rocks they are called rocky shores. The rocks create a lot of hiding places for animals.

Tide pools

When the tide goes out, water is trapped between the rocks. This creates tide pools, cut off from the sea until the tide returns.

Rock shelters

Tide pools are miniature worlds. They provide shelter for plenty of animals, such as starfish (left), snails, crabs, and barnacles. Some seaweeds also live in tide pools.

4

Coastal creatures

Marine iguanas live in the cold Pacific Ocean around the Galápagos Islands. They are reptiles, which means that they are cold-blooded creatures. They come out of the water and sunbathe on the rocks to warm up.

Seaweed

Seaweeds cling to the rocks surrounding the pools. Small animals, such as crabs, snails, and fish, hide among the seaweed.

Did you know?

The blenny, a small tide-pool fish, is sometimes called the sea-frog because it likes to sunbathe on the rocks. It jumps back into the water with a plop if it is disturbed.

Blenny fish

Sandy shores

Tiny grains of sand are made as waves batter rocks into smaller and smaller pieces. Tides carry the sand along the coast and wash it up on the shore to form sandy beaches.

Traveling coconuts

Coconut palms are a common sight on tropical beaches. When coconuts drop into the sea, they are carried by the tide to other beaches—where they grow into new palms.

Sand colonies

Soft, sandy beaches are perfect places for many sea creatures, such as seals (above), to give birth. Seals raise their young in large groups on the beaches.

Behind the beach

Winds from the sea blow sand inland. Small piles of sand soon build up around obstacles, such as fences, plants, and stones. The piles of sand become gradually larger and, eventually, a sand dune is formed.

Did you know? Sand dunes are gradually blown inland by the wind. In some parts of France, sand dunes have buried whole villages.

Seashells

Many sea animals have shells. When these animals die, their soft body rots away, leaving behind the shell. Empty shells are often washed ashore. Shells of many different shapes and sizes can be found on beaches.

Polyps

Tiny builders

Reefs are made by groups of tiny coral animals that live together. Each tiny coral animal is called a polyp. A polyp (left) has a tubelike body and a ring of tentacles around its mouth.

Living reef

Coral reefs are built by hard corals. These are coral animals that leave behind a stony skeleton when they die. Their skeletons create a habitat in which other animals can live.

Feather star

Feather stars (below) are related to starfish, and live on the coral reef. They have a cup-shaped body and many feathery arms. The arms are covered in a sticky substance that traps small animals as they float by.

Feather star

Living in crevices

Many animals, such as the moray eel (right), hide in the cracks and crevices on the reef. The moray eel darts out and grabs any small fish that swim too close.

Sponges

Sponges are animals, but they do not move around. Some sponges grow to about 6½ feet tall. Others form a flat, crustlike growth over the surface of the reef.

Vase sponges

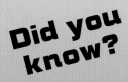

Did you know?

There are more than 5,000 different types of sponge. Some of the largest may be many hundreds of years old.

Jellyfish

Jellyfish are not actually fish. They are invertebrates with a jellylike body, and are related to corals and sea anemones.

Floating bells

Jellyfish have a soft, bell-shaped body with tentacles hanging beneath the bell. Each tentacle is covered in cells that can sting or kill other creatures.

This jellyfish has tentacles —————— covered in stinging cells.

Underwater moons

Most jellyfish float in the water and are carried around by currents. Some can swim very slowly by squeezing water in and out of their bell—which looks a little like an umbrella opening and closing.

Lion's mane

The largest jellyfish is the lion's mane. Its bell is more than 3 feet across and the tentacles are many feet long. They eat almost anything that bumps into their tentacles.

Sea nettles

Sea nettles (below) are a small type of jellyfish. Each year, in some parts of the world, swarms of sea nettles gather together to lay eggs. Sea nettles can sting, so people and marine animals stay away from these areas.

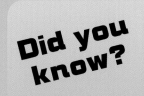

Did you know?

Each year, more people are killed by jellyfish than by the more feared great white sharks.

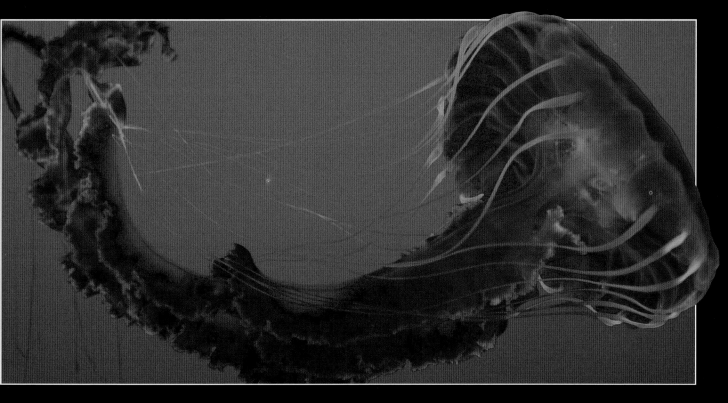

Hunters

Large hunting fish, such as sharks, swordfish, and marlin, are at the top of the ocean food chain. These fearsome fish are designed for hunting.

The dorsal fin forms a crest along the back of the fish.

Marlin

The marlin (right) is related to the tuna and swordfish. It is a large fish with a spearlike snout. It hunts alone, swimming in the surface waters of the ocean in search of fish and squid.

Swordfish

The swordfish (above) is named after its long, swordlike snout. It does not spear its prey, but moves its "sword" from side to side to slice them up. It swims alone and is often seen leaping out of the water.

Sailfish

These fish have a large, sail-like fin along their back. They use it to gather together groups of fish and squid, which they then eat. Sailfish can fold back the fin to create a sleek, streamlined shape for swimming.

Did you know?

Sailfish are the fastest swimming fish. They have an amazing top speed of 70 miles per hour.

Mako shark

The mako is a muscular fish with a tail fin shaped for speed. It can swim at up to 20 miles an hour. It has sharp teeth, which it uses to grip slippery prey, such as tuna and mackerel.

Giant fish

Some creatures found in the oceans are huge. These include whales and fish, such as basking sharks, disk-shaped sunfish, and winged manta rays.

Manta ray

A manta ray (right) usually swims slowly through the ocean, but when threatened by hunters, such as sharks, it leaps out of the water in an attempt to escape.

The wings of a manta ray can be up to 23 feet wide.

Ocean-going shark

The white-tipped shark grows to about 13 feet long. It usually swims slowly just below the surface, but sometimes sticks its nose out of the water to sniff the air in search of food.

Wahoo

The wahoo (above) can grow up to 5½ feet long. It is nicknamed the "striped rocket" because of its missile-shaped body and its habit of leaping out of the water with its prey in its jaws.

Did you know?

The average length of a sunfish is about 6 feet, but some have been found that are 10 feet long.

Sun bather

The sunfish has an unusual shape—it is almost circular when seen from the side, with fins sticking out of the top and bottom of its body. Sunfish feed on jellyfish, and can weigh more than 4,500 pounds.

Ocean turtles

Many turtles make long journeys across the oceans in search of food. They return to the beach where they were born to lay their eggs.

Growing up

Turtles spend the first few years of their life in the open ocean. They feed on jellyfish and other animals there before returning to coastal waters to mate.

Green turtle

Turtles have flat flippers to help them swim.

Green turtles

Green turtles are expert swimmers with a smooth, streamlined shell and flippers. They are the largest hard-shelled turtle in the ocean. They grow to 3 feet across, and weigh over 400 pounds. Baby green turtles are meat eaters, but adults feed on sea grass.

Hawksbill turtles

This rare turtle gets its name from the birdlike shape of its head. It spends as long as 20 years at sea before it is ready to breed. Sadly, it is killed for its attractive shell, which is used to make jewelry and ornaments.

Toothless turtles

All turtles are toothless. Instead of teeth, they use their beaks to crush coral and crabs, or graze on sea grass. Their head, like the rest of their body, is covered with small scales.

Toothless beak of a hawksbill turtle

Did you know?

Some green turtles feed off the coast of Brazil and swim across the Atlantic to breed on Ascension Island—a round journey of about 2,800 miles.

Dolphins

The dolphin is one of the most intelligent animals in the ocean. This playful marine mammal uses sound to find its prey, and lives in groups.

The bottlenose dolphin can spin in the air before landing back in the water.

Leaping dolphins

The acrobatic dolphin moves its powerful tail up and down to build up enough speed to jump out of the water. Dolphins often leap into the air while chasing fish to eat.

Hunting with sound

Dolphins use sound to find their prey. This is called echolocation. They make whistling and clicking sounds, which travel through the water. These sounds bounce off any prey in the water, creating echoes that the dolphins can hear.

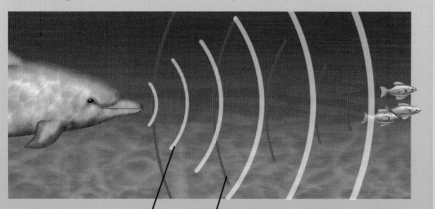

Sound waves made by dolphin.

Echoes tell the dolphin the shape, size, and location of their prey.

Looking after baby

A female dolphin gives birth to her calf, or baby, under the water. The mother pushes her calf to the surface so it can take its first breath. The calf feeds on its mother's milk for about a year.

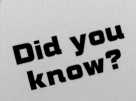

Did you know?

Dolphins do not sleep because they have to come to the surface to breathe, but they do rest at the water's surface for a few minutes at a time.

Living together

Dolphins live together in groups called pods. A pod usually contains about 10 to 12 dolphins, but super pods of thousands of dolphins are formed when pods join up.

Ocean ice

The surfaces of the polar oceans are covered by ice during the winter. As temperatures fall, the sea freezes, forming a thick layer of ice called an ice sheet.

Sheets of ice

Fresh water freezes at 32 degrees Fahrenheit, but the salt water of the polar oceans freezes at 28 degrees Fahrenheit. The thick sheet of ice formed at the surface is not flat. Strong winds push the sheets of ice together to form ridges.

Life under the ice

Sea ice forms a protective layer, beneath which live many animals. These include Arctic cod and smaller animals, such as krill and copepods. These animals attract hungry predators, such as seals (above).

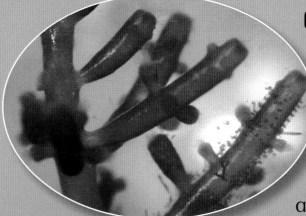

Growing on ice

Sea ice is not solid like a block of ice. It is crisscrossed with small channels filled with salty water. Tiny living things, such as algae (left), bacteria, and copepods, live in these channels. Sometimes there are so many red algae that the ice is a red color.

Breaking up ice

In spring, when temperatures rise, the ice sheet breaks up into large chunks called floes. These get smaller and smaller as they are moved around by the ocean currents.

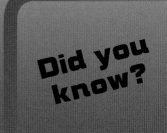

Did you know?

The Arctic is the least salty ocean in the world. This is because the lack of warm sunshine means that less water evaporates than elsewhere.

Many polar animals, such as seals and penguins, pull themselves out of the water on to the sea ice to rest.

Polar whales

Most whales, including the humpback, visit polar waters only to feed. But some whales, such as belugas, spend all year in the chilly Arctic.

White whale

The beluga (left) is a white whale found in the Arctic. It is very noisy and talks to other belugas using a range of sounds, including whistles and squeaks.

Polar unicorns

Male narwhals have an unusual spiral tusk. The tusk is actually a very long tooth. These whales (right) are rubbing their tusks together. This is not aggression, but is a way of communicating with each other.

Looking for prey

The massive orca, or killer whale (below), hunts in polar waters, feeding on animals, such as fish, squid, penguins, and seals. Orcas often hunt together. When they see penguins or seals resting on a small ice floe, one orca tips over the ice while the others wait to catch the prey.

The orca is easy to recognize by its black and white markings.

Trapped by ice

In winter, ice extends quickly over the water, and whales that are feeding in bays or between large floes can get trapped. They die if their breathing holes in the ice close up.

Did you know?

In 1978, five humpback whales and one narwhal were trapped by ice in a bay in Newfoundland, Canada. For two months, people kept breathing holes open for the whales until the ice melted and they could escape.

23

Acknowledgments

All artwork supplied by Peter Bull, The Art Agency.

Photo credits:
b—bottom, t—top, r—right, l—left, m—middle

Cover: Front—Tim Davis/Corbis, back—Stephen Frink/GettyImages, Jeff Hunter/GettyImages.

Poster: Poster: Tim Davis/Corbis.

Internals:
1 Dreamstime.com/Mikhail Blajenov, 2–3 Stuart Westmorland/Corbis, 4b Dreamstime.com/Publicimage, 5tl Dreamstime.com,
5r Dreamstime.com/Michael Johnson Jr, 6–7 Dreamstime.com/Mikhail Matsonashvili, 6br Dreamstime.com/Dmitry Pichugin,
7t Dreamstime.com/Elena Elisseeva, 7b Dreamstime.com/Nikolay Dimitrov, 8tl NOAA, 8b Dreamstime.com/Asther Lau Choon Siew,
9t Dreamstime.com/John Abramo, 9b Dreamstime.com/John Anderson, 10t Dreamstime.com/Cathy Figuli,
10b Dreamstime.com/Nick Edens, 11 tr Kip Evans, 11b Dreamstime.com/Alexei Novikov, 12–13 Bob Gomel/CORBIS,
12cl istockphoto.com/Luis Carlos Torres, 13t NOAA, 13b Dreamstime.com/Roman Dekan, 14–15 Amos Nachoum/CORBIS,
14bl Dreasmtime.com/Martin Strmko, 15tr istockphoto.com/Chuck Babbitt, 15br NOAA, 16t Digital Vision,
16b Dreamstime.com/Tommy Schultz, 17tr Digital Vision, 17b Dreamstime.com/David Lloyd, 18tr istockphoto.com/Kristian Sekulic,
18–19 Stuart Westmorland/CORBIS, 20t Dreamstime.com, 20bl Rick Price/CORBIS, 21tl NOAA,
21b Dreamstime.com/Natalia Bratslavsky, 22tl istockphoto.com/Klaas Lingbeek van Kranen, 22b NOAA.